A VERY COMMON PROCEDURE

BY COURTNEY BARON

D1564300

★

★

DRAMATISTS
PLAY SERVICE
INC.

For Christian Parker, Tyler Marchant and Amy Wegener. Thank you for your dedication.

A VERY COMMON PROCEDURE recieved its New York premiere by MCC Theater (Robert LuPone, Artistic Director; Bernard Telsey, Artistic Director; William Cantler, Associate Artistic Director) at the Lucille Lortel Theatre on February 14, 2007. It was directed by Michael Greif; the set design was by Robin Vest; the costume design was by Miranda Hoffman; the lighting design was by Tyler Micoleau; the original music and sound design were by Fabian Obispo; the production stage manager was Amy McCraney; and production manager was BD White. The cast was as follows:

DR. ANIL PATEL .... Amir Arison
CAROLYN GOLDENHERSCH .... Lynn Collins
MICHAEL GOLDENHERSCH .... Stephen Kunken

CHARACTERS

CAROLYN GOLDENHERSCH, early 30s
MICHAEL GOLDENHERSCH, early 30s
DR. ANIL PATEL, early 30s

Note: Standalone dashes in dialogue indicate a nonverbal response.

A VERY COMMON PROCEDURE

Carolyn stands next to Anil. Lights up.

CAROLYN. Oh god. Do you recognize me? This is what I keep asking myself. Am I familiar? Let's be familiar. Know each other. No, let's be honest. Know me. That's all I'm saying. And for God's sake: Really see me. I want you to. Seriously. *(She laughs.)* This isn't a joke. *(She contains herself.)* This is what I do: He stands so close. I cup his face in my hands. His face has come to mean so much to me — a replacement. For the thing my husband and I have lost. More than a baby. Much more than that. And his skin, it's … Well, it's … And he is … And he says:

ANIL. Love me.

CAROLYN. And of course. Of course. *(A long moment. Carolyn kisses Anil. It's a perfect, tender kiss.)* It isn't a dream. And it isn't infidelity, I love my husband. It's something else. *(She giggles uncomfortably.)* I confess. I have sexual fantasies — true — and — I — ha! — I masturbate to the thought of having sex with the doctor who killed my baby. *(She smiles. Her husband, Michael, appears.)* Hey, we're all learning. Ha. I love my husband. Right, Michael, learning. Ha. All of the time. It's the thing. The substance of life.

MICHAEL. We chose a teaching hospital. They say, some people — maybe you, maybe some of you say that you can get the best care at a teaching hospital. That the teachers want to show how to do it right, that there's more money for research, a better checks and balance system.

CAROLYN. We're all learning, right? We learn to lift our heads, to crawl, to walk, to speak. To spell our names. To multiply. To divide. To perform a balloon catheterization on the heart of a premature infant —

MICHAEL. Someone has to learn how.

CAROLYN. Has to practice on an infant?

MICHAEL. Yes. Has to practice on an infant.

CAROLYN. I do know he's right.

MICHAEL. I'm always right.

CAROLYN. Really?

MICHAEL. Definitely. They should know this now, it will make things simpler. I'm always right. Just so you know.

CAROLYN. Now they know.

MICHAEL. Alright. You can go on.

CAROLYN. The doctor tells us, in the hospital, that the procedure that he performed on our — that there was a complication.

MICHAEL. We know he is a fellow, he is introduced to us as a fellow. And then he tells us, tells Carolyn really, later tells her, when I'm in the hall.

CAROLYN. Why were you in the hall?

MICHAEL. He tells Carolyn. He tells her that there was a complication. That the procedure he performed didn't —

CAROLYN. No. It didn't.

MICHAEL. He's so young.

CAROLYN. He's our age.

MICHAEL. We're so young.

CAROLYN. Not anymore.

MICHAEL. She's right. You think it happens when you get married — but really, the gray hairs, they only barely sprout with marriage. But when your wife says:

CAROLYN. I'm pregnant.

MICHAEL. Full bloom. The gray garden. She says:

CAROLYN. I'm sure. I've gone to the doctor. Taken the test.

MICHAEL. Gray forest.

CAROLYN. Well?

MICHAEL. I'm shocked.

CAROLYN. You can't be too shocked —

MICHAEL. I can't?

CAROLYN. Honey, all I've got is the eggs —

MICHAEL. Right.

CAROLYN. Are you happy?

MICHAEL. Am I happy?

CAROLYN. Yes, Michael, are you happy that we're pregnant?

MICHAEL. I'm pregnant?

CAROLYN. We're going to have a baby.

MICHAEL. We're going to have a baby.

CAROLYN. Be proud Michael, you've got swimmers.

MICHAEL. And I am. My hair turns gray. I've never been so proud in my life. I ask Carolyn to call me "dad" to test it out.

CAROLYN. I can't call you dad.

MICHAEL. My mother calls my dad "father."

CAROLYN. Exactly.

MICHAEL. So, I call my brother. I make him start calling me "Dad" for a couple of weeks. Then we try "Pa."

CAROLYN. Pa? Ma and Pa Goldenhersch? What is that like Jew-billy?

MICHAEL. Actually, I think a lot about my parents. It's hard to tell them when Carolyn gets pregnant. It's hard because in that moment, somehow, I can't help but become them. I become them because I become a parent.

CAROLYN. We call a meeting of families. We don't want anyone to feel left out. We want to tell our parents at once. We've sworn secrecy up until this moment. We decide to do it over a meal: brunch. Brunch seems like the best time to discuss pregnancy, dinner seemed too, too what? What did we say?

MICHAEL. I think we said that dinner was too adult.

CAROLYN. Did we really?

MICHAEL. Yes.

CAROLYN. So we meet for eggs.

MICHAEL. To announce the egg.

CAROLYN. Michael and I both order pancakes.

MICHAEL. We've made the egg joke on the train on the way to brunch and it doesn't seem so cute to actually eat them when we get to the restaurant.

CAROLYN. In fact, through my whole pregnancy, I can't eat eggs.

MICHAEL. And I can't eat sperm.

CAROLYN. Charming. So, we arrive at the restaurant first.

MICHAEL. Carolyn is chronically early. It's a pain in the ass living with her when everyone else is always ten minutes late. So we wait twenty.

CAROLYN. My mother arrives next. I remember she looked pretty that day. Like she, I don't know, she looked pretty in her knit brunch suit. It had gold toggle buttons against a kind of lemony color, yellowish —

9

MICHAEL. She looked eggy.

CAROLYN. —

MICHAEL. And what else? Your mom shows up with a gift.

CAROLYN. Followed by your mom and dad. Also with gift.

MICHAEL. Baby gifts.

CAROLYN. Which is curious because you weren't supposed to have told your parents yet.

MICHAEL. Back at you.

CAROLYN. We were hopeless.

MICHAEL. I think it will be different if — when we do it again. That we'd keep it to ourselves. For just a little while longer. The second you're outed, that's it —

CAROLYN. You become the parents of the yet-born child. All the rest of your identity is brushed to the wayside.

MICHAEL. There's no easing into your new identity. That's it. You're parents.

CAROLYN. And then you're not. *(Anil appears.)*

ANIL. This was a vaginal delivery, thirty-two weeks. Four pounds two ounces. Seventeen inches long. Baby girl Goldenhersch born with an *apgar* score of five. Shortly after birth the baby exhibited signs of cyanosis and was subsequently diagnosed with d-transposition. A Rashkind procedure or a transcatheter balloon atrial septostomy was performed by myself, under the supervision of my senior attending.

CAROLYN. Falling in love is something to behold. This is what I think. Falling in love is living. Really living. Dr. Anil Patel. The object of my affections.

ANIL. I realize she is following me. I've announced the death of their child and she follows me down the hall to the elevator. She doesn't catch up to me. I press the button for the elevator. I have the feeling that I shouldn't turn around and say anything. The elevator comes. The doors open. I step inside and turn around. I am facing her. The doors start to close. She puts out her arm and stops them. She stands there, staring at me. She pulls back her arm. The elevator doors close. That's it.

CAROLYN. My mother always told me to marry a doctor. Instead, I married a copy writer.

MICHAEL. My father always told me to marry a Jew who looks like a shiksa.

CAROLYN. Is that true? What does that mean?

ANIL. During my second year of medical school, the class I hated most was Patient-Doctor … It's where you first learn to take patient's history. My first one on one, I came back with an eight-page Dickensian account of a woman's life. I still remember that she was from Akron, Ohio, but was born in Eugene, Oregon. It wasn't until I was about to turn it in that I realized that I had left out the most important part. Just before I handed it in, I scribbled: "Patient complains of chest pain." I told my professor what I had done, I was practically in tears. He said, "Anil, you'll make a fine doctor if you can stay this interested in your patients' lives." I've tried, but I have never been good with people. But now my patients are infants, not people. The babies, I understand the babies.

CAROLYN. We hold out hope. Truly, like it's this tangible object. We hold it out in front of ourselves and stare at it and wonder when it will take shape, when hope will become recognizable. It's like going to Barney's warehouse sale, all these women scrambling through the bins of Marc Jacobs cashmere T-shirts and Jill Sander sweaters and you see something in the "medium bin," it's black and looks soft. You push past Miss Too Tall Too Skinny and grab it. You hold it up, it takes form, but is it a sweater, is it a tank top, what? And then it emerges and it's actually a seventy-five-percent off Armani silk pullover. It's the jackpot. It's hope. It's hope in your hands, having just taken shape.

MICHAEL. The gift my parents brought to the "announce the baby brunch," it's indicative of the kind of people they are.

CAROLYN. That's not fair —

MICHAEL. Yes it is. I've known them for a hell of a lot longer than you have —

CAROLYN. Fine —

MICHAEL. Isn't that funny though, the way we think that it's time that determines how well we know someone? I know you better than I know my parents, better than I've ever known anyone and we've only known each other five years.

CAROLYN. We took an accelerated course. Your parents' gift.

MICHAEL. Right. My parents brought, this is good, a Steiff penguin.

CAROLYN. Tell them what it's like.

MICHAEL. It's about three inches tall and it's a collectable. It's abrasive and woolly and has little, well, little metal, torture devices for feet that would poke out any kid's eye. And it isn't that my parents thought that we could start a Stieff collection for our baby, they actually thought they were buying an age-appropriate stuffed animal.

CAROLYN. My mother brought a set of Burberry plaid sippy cups and commented how no baby should be without style. And later, after her second Bloody Mary — my mother loves brunch — she said, holding up one of the sippy cups "Wouldn't they make great flasks. You could use them in the car. Nothing would spill if you stopped short." Right after brunch, on the subway, we turn to each —

MICHAEL. Before we even get to the subway

CAROLYN. We turn to each other and say.

MICHAEL. We are not letting our parents near the baby.

CAROLYN. We are not letting our parents near the baby. Your mom and dad will set up a play station with knives and forks in the kitchen on a hot stove —

MICHAEL. While your mother spikes the bottles of breast milk with Wild Turkey.

CAROLYN. Okay, let's swear. Swear never to leave our child in the exclusive stead of our parents.

MICHAEL. I swear.

CAROLYN. This is something.

MICHAEL. It's huge.

CAROLYN. We're going to be good at this, I can tell.

MICHAEL. God, I love you.

CAROLYN. We kissed a lot during that time. I mean in public. With tongue.

MICHAEL. Like this. *(He grabs her and kisses her deeply. She pushes him away, laughing. He grabs her face. They kiss. In sync this time.)*

CAROLYN. Like that. *(Anil appears.)* I see Anil, Dr. Patel, when I first arrive on the maternity ward. Let me tell you what happened. The sequence of tragic events. On a sunny Friday in October. I'm barely eight months pregnant. I won't say that pregnancy was blissful, but it was good. I felt good. Tired and fat, but good. And I am walking down Seventh, on my way to Mommy-to-be-Yoga, it is a perfect fall day. And I'm making my way through the lunchtime crowds and I've got my yoga mat slung over my shoulder. I get a knowing look from another pregnant woman, we smile at each other and rub our bellies in solidarity. Then as I'm crossing Fifty-third, I feel a trickle. Followed by a swoosh. I know that the pressure on the bladder can make it hard to hold in pee, I had been peeing every time I sneezed for weeks, but this is different and I know it. I stop. Dead still. I do something that must have appeared utterly disgusting. I reach down, rub my hands on the fluid that's seeped through my yoga pants and I smell my hand. I am hoping that it has a pee smell, an ammonia smell. It doesn't. I try to hail a cab. I start to cry right away. Because you know. You just know. I call Michael and I say, I think something's wrong. He says:

MICHAEL. What's wrong?

CAROLYN. I don't know. I think I'm wet.

MICHAEL. What?

CAROLYN. Maybe, I don't know, maybe my water broke.

MICHAEL. It can't.

CAROLYN. I know.

MICHAEL. It's not time.

CAROLYN. I know.

MICHAEL. Maybe, honey, maybe you sat in something?

CAROLYN. Michael, I felt it come out of me.

MICHAEL. Do you want me to come home?

CAROLYN. No. I don't know. I'm going to go to the doctor's office.

MICHAEL. Do you want me to come?

CAROLYN. No.

MICHAEL. You're going to be fine.

CAROLYN. I know.

MICHAEL. You are.

CAROLYN. I know, I'll call you.

MICHAEL. And three hours later, I finally find her at Mount Sinai hospital. She's on her way into the delivery room. I had been at work and then went to a meeting downtown. Then on the subway. I missed her call. But I found you.

CAROLYN. You did. And our baby was born.

MICHAEL. She was.

CAROLYN. She was small.

MICHAEL. A peanut.

CAROLYN. She was a peanut.

ANIL. It is four days, maybe five, after the Goldenhersch baby died. The mother, Carolyn Goldenhersch is at the deli where I get my morning coffee. She's smiling at me. She says:

CAROLYN. Dr. Patel?

ANIL. Yes?

CAROLYN. How funny.

ANIL. Good morning.

CAROLYN. Is this where you buy your coffee?

ANIL. Every morning.

CAROLYN. How funny.

ANIL. Is it?

CAROLYN. It is. *(Pause.)* Dr. Patel?

ANIL. Yes?

CAROLYN. The coffee, the coffee here. It's terrible.

ANIL. *(Laughing.)* Always. Every day.

CAROLYN. You know there's a Starbucks around the corner.

ANIL. Sure. But the coffee here is seventy-five cents. I don't much like it in the first place.

CAROLYN. Then why drink it?

ANIL. Caffeine. Habit.

CAROLYN. Dr. Patel?

ANIL. Yes?

CAROLYN. You don't recognize me, do you?

ANIL. From the hospital.

CAROLYN. Yes. From the hospital.

ANIL. —

CAROLYN. Will you come around the corner with me. Have Starbucks?

ANIL. I really can't.

CAROLYN. My treat.

ANIL. Carolyn Goldenhersch is pretty.

CAROLYN. You look like you could use a latté.

ANIL. Carolyn Goldenhersch has a lovely smile.

CAROLYN. Live a little.

ANIL. Okay. Sure. Yes. Thank you.

CAROLYN. Good. Okay. Yes. Great.

ANIL. Starbucks is very crowded. I don't let her pay. I spend eight dollars on two coffees. Eight dollars. My deli is bad, but coffee is seventy-five cents. We didn't drink coffee in my house growing up. My mother had tea every now and then and my father drank diet sodas. Starting with Fresca, then Tab. He'd sidle up to breakfast with Tab in one hand and say, "Anil. Tab is for the beautiful people." That was the campaign then. Tab: for beautiful people.

CAROLYN. I wanted to see you.

ANIL. You did?

CAROLYN. Mmm-hmm. I did. Do you know why I wanted to see you?

ANIL. No. I have no idea.

CAROLYN. Exactly. Dr. Patel for five days I have wanted to see you, but I don't know why. Why do you think it could be?

ANIL. Maybe you have some questions?

CAROLYN. No. I don't think so. You look much taller in the hospital.

ANIL. I wear clogs.

CAROLYN. Oh.

ANIL. They have a little lift to them. Today I'm wearing loafers.

CAROLYN. You'll change into your clogs at the hospital?

ANIL. Yes.

CAROLYN. You have a locker or something at the hospital?

ANIL. Yes.

CAROLYN. Like at the gym.

ANIL. Exactly. Carolyn Goldenhersch should drink Tab.

CAROLYN. Are you friends with any of your patients?

ANIL. My patients are infants.

CAROLYN. Right. The parents aren't patients, are they? The babies. But the parents. Are you friends with any of them?

ANIL. No.

CAROLYN. No. With other doctors, are you friends with the other doctors?

ANIL. Some.

CAROLYN. Many.

ANIL. I don't know about many.

CAROLYN. More than five?

ANIL. What kind of friends?

CAROLYN. More than hello, go out for a drink, have dinner. Movies.

ANIL. No.

CAROLYN. No. Are you married?

ANIL. No.

CAROLYN. Girlfriend?

ANIL. Mrs. Goldenhersch …

CAROLYN. Carolyn.

ANIL. Carolyn.

CAROLYN. Yes?

ANIL. Where are you leading me?

CAROLYN. Do you feel like I'm leading you?

ANIL. Yes.

CAROLYN. Are you following?

MICHAEL. Old people die. This is the way I must have always thought, because when our baby died, I wasn't just upset, or sad, or angry, I was honestly perplexed. Indignant even. Babies don't die. This is what I thought. Babies don't die. I am walking around a lot. Taking those pensive strolls that I've heard about but never needed before. Never needed to get air. I've been volunteering at Bide-a-Wee, it's like a low rent ASPCA. I've been walking the dogs for an hour around lunch time. I always walk the oldest dog. I swear he's fourteen. Old and huge and smells. No one will adopt this dog. I want to bring him home and care for him as he dies. Because he's going to die. Sooner rather than later. Big dogs don't live as long as little dogs. When your baby dies in the hospital on the operating table. When that happens. When that happens. It's unspeakable. When it happens you aren't there. You don't give the only thing you can give, you can't comfort, you can't lovingly pet her head and let her slip away knowing she's loved. You can't. Not in a hospital, when she's in the other room. On the table. Knocked out. Drugged. You can't do anything. Can't be a father. The dog. That's something. I understand it. I see it. I should care for this dog while it dies. It would be right. I should bring him home. I should. I should do something. Everything is shit.

CAROLYN. Good luck to you, Dr. Anil Patel.

ANIL. Are we done here?

CAROLYN. I think so.

ANIL. My best to your husband.

CAROLYN. Your best.

ANIL. Yes, and to you.

CAROLYN. Thank you.

ANIL. And that's it. We have coffee in Starbucks. And that's it.

CAROLYN. He offered me his best. I believed him. His best. His best did not save our daughter. Maybe his best is simply not good enough.

MICHAEL. There are doctors at the top of their class. Then there have to be those at the bottom of their class, right? A doctor at the bottom of the class? I wasn't at the top of my class. I am not, however, a doctor. I'm a copy writer. I got a good job straight out of school, based not on grades, but on, what? Promise? When Carolyn and I met, she said something like, "You will always succeed at being you." I know she meant that I would never get past my own limitations.

CAROLYN. I said, "You are so successful at being yourself." I meant that you are true to yourself and then, back then, before he began to rework parts of our history into a path of skepticism and regret, back then when I said, "You are so successful at being yourself." He said:

MICHAEL. That's the nicest thing anyone ever said to me.

CAROLYN. I mean it. It's like you know who you are and you accept it with such admirable intensity.

MICHAEL. I love getting to know you.

CAROLYN. Really?

MICHAEL. My last girlfriend, she didn't want to get to know me. She wanted to change the way I dress.

CAROLYN. Did she?

MICHAEL. No.

CAROLYN. I want to warn you —

MICHAEL. What?

CAROLYN. I might try to take you shopping.

MICHAEL. Is it that bad?

CAROLYN. Michael, that's a lot of brown.

MICHAEL. I like brown.

CAROLYN. You look like a Cocoa Puff.

MICHAEL. I'm successfully being me.

CAROLYN. Yeah?

MICHAEL. I want to successfully be me kissing you. What do you think?

CAROLYN. I'm coo-coo for Cocoa Puffs. *(They kiss. Carolyn pulls away.)*

MICHAEL. Was that our first date?

CAROLYN. Our first official date.

MICHAEL. We had unofficial ones?

CAROLYN. Sure. The pre-date coffee date. The late-night phone call pre-date. Then the first date. The one where you asked me out. Where you said, "Go out with me on Friday." Where you planned the date.

MICHAEL. It was a good first date, don't you think?

CAROLYN. A walk across the Brooklyn Bridge to Grimaldi's for pizza. It was a great first date Michael. First dates are always great.

ANIL. I know I shouldn't, but I agree to take her for Indian food in Jackson Heights, Queens. It's a predominately Indian neighborhood. She doesn't want to stay in Manhattan. I think she's afraid of being seen in her own borough. Actually she takes me for Indian. The Jackson Heights Diner doesn't take credit cards and at the end of the meal I realize I don't have cash. After dinner we walk around. She drags me into all of the sari stores.

CAROLYN. I wear too much black.

ANIL. You look very New York.

CAROLYN. I want to look very something else.

ANIL. Like what? Very Idaho?

CAROLYN. I want to look very Indian.

ANIL. I buy her a sari. The woman at the shop shows her how to put it on. The woman at the shop thinks we're getting married. And on the subway home she says:

CAROLYN. Tell me what it's like to be Hindu.

ANIL. I can't.

CAROLYN. Why not? It's sacred? Forbidden to tell a Jew?

ANIL. I'm an atheist.

MICHAEL. When Carolyn and I got married, my Great Aunt Birdie from Ohio sent us shabbat candlesticks. We relegated them to the regifting pile — I want to use them now. On Friday nights I want to find God. Be thankful for something, have a history that takes us back farther than the day when our baby died —

CAROLYN. We were born on that day.

MICHAEL. She actually believes that. Actually believes that we've been wrapped up in a Christian myth of resurrection. That we died for our sins and were resurrected as what? Martyrs? Is that right? Saints of the Lost Baby?

CAROLYN. He's so caught up in the placement of words. He always loved Phillip Roth a little too much for my taste —

MICHAEL. And what do you read? Who are your authors?

CAROLYN. I read.

MICHAEL. No Carolyn, you *read*, past tense, read. Carolyn read Sylvia Plath's *The Bell Jar* and thought it would be fun to get an internship at *Vogue* or *Bazaar*. She's never really read.

CAROLYN. And what does that mean?

MICHAEL. You don't get it. It means that you don't see the

importance of the story being told. We learn from the lives that are presented to us through literature.

CAROLYN. What do we learn from our story, Michael?

MICHAEL. No. I mean they learn. The audience learns.

CAROLYN. What are you teaching them?

MICHAEL. *This, this* is what I'm teaching them: If you ever, dear audience, know anyone who loses a baby and you know them well, don't send a card. If you know them well, take them to dinner. After the baby died, people sent cards. Sympathy cards. No one offered to take us to dinner. Maybe if we had gone out, right away, if we hadn't sequestered ourselves in our grief, maybe then — if we had gone out. Together, if we had gone out together. Instead we isolated ourselves. Separated. I need my wife. I process everything through her. If you had taken us to dinner, if you had forced us to share a meal. Instead, when you send a card, it's as good as saying, "I can't be there for you."

CAROLYN. I liked the cards.

MICHAEL. You never looked at the cards.

CAROLYN. I'd like every person here to send us a sympathy card.

MICHAEL. No you wouldn't.

CAROLYN. Yes, I would.

ANIL. *(To the audience.)* I'm a liar. When I take Carolyn to Jackson Heights for a little Indian culture, I'm a liar. I was born here, grew up here, I've been to India, but it isn't who I am. I let it define me when I'm with Carolyn, she thinks it's exotic, that I'm special. That I am foreign and therefore interesting. But, I am a racist against my parent's culture, I make it something other. I say, "Isn't Indian culture strange, you white people." And, "Oh yes, we all smell of curry, but we're very good with computers and we smile a lot."

MICHAEL. When I said — about the cards. I'm sorry. The gesture, I didn't mean to say that they weren't — that they weren't sent with good intentions — really. I didn't mean. I'm sorry.

CAROLYN. What else do you do?

ANIL. What do you mean?

CAROLYN. You're at the hospital, then you go home, what else?

ANIL. I don't have time for anything else.

CAROLYN. All I have is time.

ANIL. That must be nice.

CAROLYN. What? No, it's awful.

19

ANIL. But you're smiling.

CAROLYN. No, I know, all of the time. It isn't right.

ANIL. It's not wrong.

CAROLYN. I can tell you that smiling is not the appropriate response to the life I'm living.

ANIL. Maybe I'm making you smile?

CAROLYN. *(With some honesty here.)* You're making me nervous.

ANIL. I am not, nor have I ever been married. When I say this aloud or to myself, I'm always surprised. Surprised because I am a young, not unattractive doctor. My mother cries every time I call home. Hears my voice and begins to weep. "Anil! You will never have a wife! You're going to die alone!" She'd say I was exaggerating, but I'm not. My mother wonders what happened to the daughter of my father's best friend's sister. The nice law student that my parents introduced me to during a winter vacation after my third semester of med school. We ice skated together in that cliché cinematic way that you fall all over each other and share hot chocolate in the car. We talked for hours.

CAROLYN. A perfect first date?

ANIL. Yes. And we dated almost every night for the month of break. Talked about ending up in the same city. She was in law school in Chicago.

CAROLYN. She was pretty?

ANIL. Yes.

CAROLYN. Indian?

ANIL. Yes.

CAROLYN. And what happened?

ANIL. We emailed for months. Met a couple of weekends. I flew to Chicago. We spent our spring break together. I wanted to marry her.

CAROLYN. Did she want to marry you?

ANIL. She said she did.

CAROLYN. You asked her?

ANIL. I asked her if she wanted to.

CAROLYN. You proposed?

ANIL. No. I just asked her if she would want to if I asked her.

CAROLYN. Isn't that a proposal?

ANIL. It was a hypothetical question.

CAROLYN. A hypothetical proposal, how romantic.

ANIL. We were going to wait, until she graduated.

CAROLYN. What happened when she graduated?

ANIL. She wanted to wait until she passed the bar.

CAROLYN. In Chicago?

ANIL. Yes.

CAROLYN. What happened after she passed the bar?

ANIL. She didn't.

CAROLYN. Oh.

ANIL. She didn't pass the bar and she called me and I said, "Try again."

CAROLYN. Did she?

ANIL. No.

CAROLYN. What did she do?

ANIL. She moved to India.

CAROLYN. Just like that?

ANIL. Yes.

CAROLYN. Did you love her?

ANIL. I think so.

CAROLYN. Is that like hypothetical love?

ANIL. It killed me.

CAROLYN. But here you are.

ANIL. You know what I mean.

CAROLYN. Yes, I know. I know because you're killing me, Dr. Patel.

ANIL. Is that so, Mrs. Goldenhersch?

CAROLYN. Yes. *(Carolyn leans in too close for Anil's comfort. They hold, close.)*

MICHAEL. I want to have another baby. I'm looking at fathers with envy. I'm suffering. I'm not reading Phillip Roth anymore. I'm reading John Grisham — reading just until the last chapter or the last couple of chapters — I don't want things to be revealed. I don't want the mysteries to be solved. I want things without ends. I want to live in the middle of the stories. I miss my wife.

CAROLYN. *(Pulling away from Anil.)* When I think about medicine, doctors, I have always had the typical Western view, the deification of the white coat. And then at some point during this whole ordeal somebody says to me the phrase "practicing medicine." And the word "practice" sticks out. I think, "Oh shit. Practice. They've been practicing medicine. Rehearsing medicine." I know I'm playing with semantics, but then you get it. Somebody has to learn.

ANIL. I hold a coveted fellowship. It's not just being smart and good, it's being the smartest, the best. It isn't arrogance. It is simply true, confirmed by acceptance into this program. This isn't a defensive remark, it's so you understand, fully, who I am.

CAROLYN. What's that smell?

MICHAEL. I'm cooking.

CAROLYN. Really? You don't cook.

MICHAEL. I do tonight.

CAROLYN. I want to go out.

MICHAEL. But I'm cooking.

CAROLYN. What are you cooking?

MICHAEL. What's your favorite food?

CAROLYN. You're making profiteroles?

MICHAEL. Lasagna.

CAROLYN. What's the occasion?

MICHAEL. Does a husband need an occasion to woo his wife?

CAROLYN. Are you wooing me?

MICHAEL. Woo-woo.

CAROLYN. You should have cooked for me when we first met, ladies love that.

MICHAEL. I had to catch you before I could poison you.

CAROLYN. I see.

MICHAEL. I think we should sign up for a cooking class.

CAROLYN. Now?

MICHAEL. Sure. We can weep while learning knife techniques together.

CAROLYN. Cry over onions.

MICHAEL. Come sit for a minute.

CAROLYN. I'm sorry, the smell, it's making me …

MICHAEL. Sick?

CAROLYN. A little. Yes.

MICHAEL. You want to go out to eat?

CAROLYN. I'm not hungry.

MICHAEL. More for me.

CAROLYN. More for you.

MICHAEL. *(A sad little attempt.)* More and more and more.

CAROLYN. Michael. Give me a little space.

MICHAEL. Sure. Sorry.

CAROLYN. It's okay. *(Pause.)* Do you think we're going to get through this?

MICHAEL. I hope so.

CAROLYN. You hope so. Yeah, I know you do.

ANIL. In reality, I'm wrong in the world. Awkward. I don't think you see that here, because Carolyn Goldenhersch does not see it.

CAROLYN. The truth is that you, *you* may be somebody's first patient. When I think about it, I can't decide if I want to know everything I can about medicine or nothing at all. Should I read up on what happened to our baby? Should I understand the procedures in greater detail? Should I ask Anil? Is that why I met him for dinner in Jackson Heights? Is that why I keep walking across the park to stand in front of the hospital? Is that why I almost kiss him? Is that why I think that I'm falling in love? All I know is that three weeks after the death of our baby, I'm going on my second date with Dr. Anil Patel. Oh, and here is the other thing, I have been trying not to lose any of the weight I gained during my pregnancy. I'm hungry all of the time. Eating all of the time. But it isn't working. I'm barely soft. I didn't gain that much. Maybe I should have gained more.

ANIL. Hungry?

CAROLYN. Famished.

ANIL. It's embarrassing. Really. I took her to Jersey City. Just off of JFK Avenue, near Journal Square, there is an Indian neighborhood. I grew up in Hartford. I grew up in the insurance capital of America. I drove a Camaro in high school. I don't want to lie to Carolyn, but there we are sitting in front of a masala dhosa and the only thing I know about Indian food, really, is that my mother had Madhur Jaffrey's cookbook. I'm sipping a mango lhassi. Carolyn Goldenhersch wants me to be someone she never imagined knowing. She wants me to be the special Indian doctor who was present at the death of her newborn. She wants me to be extraordinary.

CAROLYN. I can't believe these wonderful neighborhoods exist and nobody knows about them.

ANIL. Not nobody, Carolyn.

CAROLYN. No of course. I just meant.

ANIL. Will you take your husband here?

CAROLYN. No. He has a delicate stomach. Looks like you could eat a jalapeño farm.

ANIL. Are you comparing us?

CAROLYN. Of course.

ANIL. Don't. You don't really want to talk about your husband, do you?

CAROLYN. I want to talk about you. I don't know about you.

ANIL. I don't know about you either.

CAROLYN. Were you there when I delivered?

ANIL. Right afterwards. Yes.

CAROLYN. Saw me splayed on the table?

ANIL. Carolyn ...

CAROLYN. Then you know more about me than I know about you. It's not exactly an equal playing field.

ANIL. Do you know, Carolyn, I keep thinking that at some point we are going to turn into a movie of the week. That you're going to pull out a knife or something and kill me.

CAROLYN. Dr. Patel, let me assure you, that you are perfectly safe with me.

ANIL. Perfectly?

CAROLYN. This won't go anywhere. I won't come after you. If I obsess, I will do it on my own time. This may be our last meal together. I will not cheat on my husband.

ANIL. No?

CAROLYN. No. This is something else.

ANIL. What is it?

CAROLYN. This? This is a train wreck.

MICHAEL. Let's talk about the eight months. The eight months where Carolyn and I ate *every* meal together. Spent every moment. Where I knew where you were and you knew where I was, not because we were keeping tabs, but because we just knew. The good, no great, eight months. Where I brought you ice cream and you said that you weren't going to be one of those kinds of pregnant women and so I ate it for you. I gained more weight than you did. Your shoes stopped fitting and you wore flip-flops with socks because your feet were cold. All the time. We had amazing sex during pregnancy. And you said it all of the time:

CAROLYN. I can't believe that you're going to be the father of our baby. I can't believe that a man who can do that to me can also be a father. I can't believe how lucky I am.

MICHAEL. And I said: I love you Carolyn Goldenhersch, mother of our child. And I tried to carry you around the house when your back got sore. And I have never been so filled with love: for you and your belly.

CAROLYN. But it changed, Michael.

MICHAEL. I know it changed.

CAROLYN. Michael is always right, and now you know everything.

MICHAEL. I know we can go forward.

CAROLYN. We are parents of a dead baby.

MICHAEL. We are not only that.

CAROLYN. What else are we?

MICHAEL. —

CAROLYN. I can't love you anymore.

MICHAEL. You don't mean that.

CAROLYN. You're right. I don't.

MICHAEL. This is insane.

CAROLYN. This or me?

MICHAEL. I know this is temporary.

CAROLYN. It's not temporary.

MICHAEL. Won't you try, even a little bit.

CAROLYN. Are you?

MICHAEL. You want me to take some time off work?

CAROLYN. Then give me what I need —

MICHAEL. Yes, good, good tell me what you need. I'm dying to give it to you.

CAROLYN. Are you that stupid?

MICHAEL. I won't hate you.

CAROLYN. Yes you will.

ANIL. Carolyn needed a doctor. That's what she said.

CAROLYN. I need a doctor.

ANIL. I am a doctor.

CAROLYN. No. You're a fellow.

ANIL. Carolyn, I am a doctor.

CAROLYN. A fellow is still in training. Still funded by the medical school. A fellow. I need a doctor. I'm sick.

ANIL. You're sick?

CAROLYN. Yes.

ANIL. What's wrong?

CAROLYN. What's wrong?

ANIL. You're sick?

CAROLYN. I have a husband at home.

ANIL. Is that what we're doing here?

CAROLYN. I go home. I always will.

ANIL. I know. You should go home. There's no reason not to.

CAROLYN. There's no reason not to.

MICHAEL. I know that we can find each other. Our apartment is only nine hundred and fifty square feet. Surely we can find each other. People survive.

CAROLYN. I know they do.

MICHAEL. Couples survive.

CAROLYN. The question of couples therapy.

MICHAEL. We had both been in therapy, in individual, at some point —

CAROLYN. I was in college.

MICHAEL. I was ten.

CAROLYN. You were ten? I didn't know that. Did I know that?

MICHAEL. Apparently I seemed sad to my parents.

CAROLYN. Sad at ten?

MICHAEL. Yes. And neither of us had ever been to couples. But, we talked a lot about going — analyzed it. Analyzed what we thought we would or could get out of it:

CAROLYN. Honesty.

MICHAEL. I'm being honest.

CAROLYN. We could gain objectivity.

MICHAEL. Be serious. No such thing.

CAROLYN. Okay, then relative objectivity.

MICHAEL. Dubious.

CAROLYN. Maybe we'd feel liberated.

MICHAEL. Dr. Freud, set me free!

CAROLYN. You don't know how everything works.

MICHAEL. Neither do you.

CAROLYN. Isn't this what you want? We'd be forced to be together for one hour a week. Forced to talk. To be in the same room.

MICHAEL. I don't want you by force. *(Beat.)* Do you miss me?

CAROLYN. Yes.

MICHAEL. Then, please, Carolyn. Every time you walk out the door, my heart breaks.

CAROLYN. It's easier to miss you than to be in the same room with you.

MICHAEL. —

CAROLYN. I don't want to hurt you.

MICHAEL. Then don't.

CAROLYN. I really don't.

MICHAEL. I know. I really know.

CAROLYN. But when I see you — when I'm with you, by you —

I want to hurt — No. It's not want. It's instinctual.

MICHAEL. You instinctively want to hurt me?

CAROLYN. Not want.

ANIL. We have our third date. They are dates. They may be other things as well, but I know they're dates.

CAROLYN. We only meet to eat. We have to eat, eating together is incidental.

ANIL. Let's eat your food.

CAROLYN. By which he means brisket cooked in schmaltz, herring creamed to death. Well it's not that way for me. It's not brisket, it's filet mignon. Not chopped liver, but fois gras. It doesn't matter. We're predicated on lies. I take him to Yonah Schimmel's Knishery on the Lower East Side.

ANIL. But that's in Manhattan.

CAROLYN. Not for me. No one I know will be down there. You have to take the F train for God's sake.

ANIL. Over potato knishes she asks me for a detailed history. And then I realize how much I want to tell it. So when Carolyn Goldenhersch asks me:

CAROLYN. Tell me about what you were like in elementary school.

ANIL. I tell her.

CAROLYN. Tell me what you were you like in middle school.

ANIL. I tell her.

CAROLYN. What you were like in high school?

ANIL. I look the same as I do now. Have the same hair cut. I went to my senior prom with friends. I drove a Camaro. It was used. I had wanted a Pontiac Fiero. Hartford is, Hartford is like the rest of America. Like the rest of everything, just richer maybe? Better funded. (*He takes a quick breath and barrels through.*) No. I want to tell you. I didn't look exactly like I do now. In high school. In high school I had terrible acne. Don't laugh. I mean terrible. Embarrassing acne. My mother took me to the doctor and actually gestured to my face and said to the doctor, "Fix him." Fix him. I used Retin-A and my skin dried up and peeled and my nose bled.

CAROLYN. Are you soliciting sympathy?

ANIL. No. Do I seem pathetic?

CAROLYN. Your nose bled. You drove a used Camaro …

ANIL. It's different than how you're saying it.

CAROLYN. How is it different?

ANIL. I'm saying that I was invisible, that I felt different. Alienated.

CAROLYN. Everyone does. You're not special.

ANIL. No. I'm not special Carolyn.

MICHAEL. My parents. They have done something so strange, so. They have invited Carolyn and me on a twenty-four-day walking tour of Indochina. My parents don't go on trips. They go on cruises. Every couple of years. They go on cruises to the Florida Keys. They rave about the performances of third-rate musical theater actors performing *Annie Get Your Gun* and the Alaskan King Crab legs from the never-empty raw bar.

CAROLYN. Twenty-four days?

MICHAEL. Yep.

CAROLYN. Where is Indochina?

MICHAEL. Really?

CAROLYN. Never mind.

MICHAEL. It's Vietnam, Cambodia. And Laos.

CAROLYN. Laos?

MICHAEL. Yes. Laos.

CAROLYN. Michael, where the hell is Laos?

MICHAEL. Indochina.

CAROLYN. Why?

MICHAEL. To be nice.

CAROLYN. It doesn't sound nice.

MICHAEL. Really?

CAROLYN. It would be with your parents.

MICHAEL. Don't be mean. They're trying to help.

CAROLYN. Help us what?

MICHAEL. Oh Jesus, Carolyn.

CAROLYN. Do you think walking around Laos with your parents will help us?

MICHAEL. We don't go to Laos. Or Vietnam. Or Cambodia. We stay in New York. If we can make it here ... Am I smiling? I intended to smile when I said that. And I told my parents that Carolyn doesn't want to travel to such a foreign place. I know that my mother will think that we are trying to get pregnant again. Put it out in the universe, right?

CAROLYN. You are ordinary.

ANIL. Are you disappointed?

CAROLYN. Of course.

ANIL. Are you special?

CAROLYN. I am now.

ANIL. Because you're dating an Indian man?

CAROLYN. Because I lost my baby.

MICHAEL. Carolyn and I do go to therapy. The first session we can barely speak. I look at her, the way you look at an animal in the zoo. In the waiting room, she reads *People* magazine.

CAROLYN. I'm on maternity leave. I told the gallery that I would take four months. One month before the birth, then three months at home. So, now, it's funny. I'm on maternity leave. I don't know where to go. I walk around. It's winter, but I'm walking around. And I see babies all day long in strollers, at playgrounds in the park, in Barnes and Nobles with nannies, with moms, all over the streets of Manhattan and I never look at them with wonder. There is no longing or sadness. I think I should mention this in therapy with Michael, but I can't. I should be, you would be, right? I know you would be. You all would be. Because it would be right to be sad.

MICHAEL. We do go to therapy. But we don't do anything else together. We don't do anything until the day she comes home with — *(Carolyn is holding a model of a heart.)*

CAROLYN. It's a heart.

MICHAEL. Yes.

CAROLYN. I bought it from a medical teaching supply catalog.

MICHAEL. Oh?

CAROLYN. It's an exact replica of an adult heart.

MICHAEL. And why do you have it?

CAROLYN. To study it. To figure it out.

MICHAEL. Is this a poetic endeavor? You're going to figure out the human heart?

CAROLYN. No. I'm going to teach me how each part works. Dr. Patel is going to give me a kind of crash course on cardiology.

MICHAEL. *(Correcting her grammar.)* In. In cardiology.

CAROLYN. Yes. In.

MICHAEL. Dr. Patel? Dr. Patel from the hospital. Why is he going to teach you? I didn't know you saw him?

CAROLYN. I want to know more about the heart.

MICHAEL. So you called Dr. Patel?

CAROLYN. He's a fellow.

MICHAEL. And you're a lass?

CAROLYN. A fellow, studying neonatal cardiology.

MICHAEL. Did you hunt him down? Harass him until he didn't have a choice?

CAROLYN. Is that what you think I'm like?

MICHAEL. You don't ever let go.

CAROLYN. Don't I?

MICHAEL. No.

CAROLYN. I think I'm letting go of some things.

MICHAEL. Don't. Just because I'm not excited that you've tracked down the doctor who told us that the baby died, don't be so cruel and pretend that you're letting me go.

CAROLYN. Michael, I want to learn about how the heart works. Dr. Patel has offered to help me. I can teach you what he teaches me.

MICHAEL. Do you really think its going to make a difference?

CAROLYN. Yes.

ANIL. *(Note: Anil should encourage the audience to make fists until they actually do.)* Make your hand into a fist. All of you, please make fists. Look at its size. Your heart is about the size of your fist. Are you surprised? As you grow, your heart grows at the same rate and size as your fist. So, an infant's heart and fist are about the same size at birth. Small.

MICHAEL. I tell my brother that I'm worried. He says, "Remember, before Carolyn you were just a bitter bastard in crap clothes." I'm remembering.

CAROLYN. I didn't mean to say that I'm special because I've lost a baby. You know better than I do, statistically, it doesn't make me special. Michael looked up the infant mortality rate. I know, babies die.

MICHAEL. Carolyn, the infant mortality rate in America was almost six in one thousand last year.

CAROLYN. Yes, Michael, I know. Babies die.

ANIL. Statistics are just statistics.

CAROLYN. I looked up the rate after Michael told me, I thought he couldn't be right. Do you know what it is in India?

ANIL. Worse.

CAROLYN. Ten times worse. Around sixty deaths to every one thousand births.

ANIL. Yes, worse.

CAROLYN. Why don't you practice medicine in India?

ANIL. Because I practice here. In my country. *(Pause.)*

CAROLYN. Do you like babies?

ANIL. Sure.

CAROLYN. Is that why you work in the NICU? Do you like babies better than adults?

ANIL. You don't choose a specialty based on who you like.

CAROLYN. Then why babies?

ANIL. Model builders. That is also what I say to my mother when she wants to know why I won't open a family practice in Hartford: model builders. The ones who make exact replicas of ships or Civil War battlefields, painstaking detail, exact replicas. But in miniature. It's the challenge of the scale. Heart surgery on a man in his forties, it's interesting, important — but think of the size of an infant's fist, that's the size of its heart. Sometimes the size of a walnut. The delicacy. Catheters aren't tubes, they're threads.

CAROLYN. Size?

ANIL. Yes. In part.

CAROLYN. You like miniatures?

ANIL. Many people do.

CAROLYN. I know a guy who breeds Wheaten Terriers. He has a whole collection of miniature Wheaten figurines.

ANIL. You're mocking me.

CAROLYN. You're mockable.

ANIL. —

CAROLYN. No, no, we're both mockable.

ANIL. I don't think you are.

CAROLYN. I am, trust me.

ANIL. Really?

CAROLYN. Yes. Fallible. Mockable. A little pathetic.

ANIL. But we're the same?

CAROLYN. Yes.

MICHAEL. I do remember Dr. Patel. He was memorable in the sea of white doctors who took care of us at the hospital. Is that racist? To point out the obvious ethnic difference of one of our doctors?

CAROLYN. Yes.

MICHAEL. Shut up. I think you should shut up.

CAROLYN. Shut up. You think I should shut up. What? Are we twelve?

MICHAEL. I remember Dr. Patel because he was Indian. Because he was the one to perform the catheterization. I remember him because the neonatologist said, "This is Dr. Patel, he'll be performing the catheterization procedure." And he said:

ANIL. I'll be performing the catheterization.

MICHAEL. Is it dangerous?

ANIL. It's a very common procedure. Sinai performs over a hundred each year.

MICHAEL. How many have you done?

ANIL. This will be my first (but) —

CAROLYN. Did he hesitate?

MICHAEL. Yes, he did. He hesitated and said:

ANIL. *(He takes a breath.)* This will be my first, but I will be supervised. Your baby will be fine.

CAROLYN. Did he promise?

ANIL. I never promise.

CAROLYN. We should have made him promise.

MICHAEL. And I held Carolyn's hand and she was still groggy from the delivery. And we started talking about names. We argued about names.

CAROLYN. Samantha?

MICHAEL. People would inevitably call her Sam. I want her to be a girl's girl. Not a little Louisa May Alcott girl.

CAROLYN. Madeleine.

MICHAEL. She's not a cookie.

CAROLYN. But the real fight was over the name Virginia.

MICHAEL. It's my favorite name.

CAROLYN. You're just in love with Virginia Woolf.

MICHAEL. She's an amazing writer, why shouldn't we name our daughter after her.

CAROLYN. Virginia Woolf committed suicide.

MICHAEL. But we didn't. Decide. We didn't name her. Didn't come to an agreement. I said, "We'll hold her and know."

CAROLYN. Do you think so?

MICHAEL. Yes.

CAROLYN. Okay.

MICHAEL. Some people do that, right? Some people wait. Wait to see what the sex of the baby is, wait to look in her eyes and know? Some of you did that, didn't you? Some of you had a name in mind, but waited. We'll hold her and know.

CAROLYN. But we didn't hold her. Didn't know. In the end, though, for paperwork, we had to name her. We had to name her something for the paperwork.

MICHAEL. We named her.

CAROLYN. Baby. Baby. How ridiculous is that. Baby Goldenhersch

MICHAEL. Like she was going to go straight from life into a 1940s slapstick comedy.

CAROLYN. Michael said:

MICHAEL. Don't give her a name. Don't name her. Don't make her a person we've lost. Don't. Just let her be. As it is. Just let it be as it is.

CAROLYN. Baby Goldenhersch.

ANIL. I want to tell you why I'm involved with Carolyn Goldenhersch. Why I'm doing something I know I shouldn't, why I'm committing this, well, unethical impropriety. I am not so naive, I know that there are lines that may be crossed. When I tell you, when I tell you what has led me to this place where I'm in a bit deeper than I had hoped. Where I wonder if I can ask her back to my apartment. When I tell you, I think you'll be disappointed. I am. Here is the truth: She needs me. And I think, I think I need her too.

CAROLYN. I told my husband that you are going to give me a crash course in cardiology.

ANIL. Okay.

CAROLYN. Okay.

ANIL. Good.

CAROLYN. Okay. Good.

ANIL. It's okay, Carolyn.

CAROLYN. Are you a good teacher.

ANIL. Yes,

CAROLYN. Okay.

ANIL. Are you hungry?

CAROLYN. Famished.

MICHAEL. After Carolyn delivered the baby, I snapped a picture with my camera phone and the baby was rushed off to the NICU. Carolyn said:

CAROLYN. Go with the baby.

MICHAEL. And I did. And before you can actually enter the NICU, you have to wash your arms and hands for literally three minutes. And as I stood there, with a nurse telling me what to do, how hot the water has to be, how to use the foot pedals to control the flow of water so that you don't have to touch anything. All of that time, I thought about how I wasn't at all prepared for a baby. How she would look up at me and she would miraculously be able to say: "Oh shit, not you." And so I went into the NICU. A nurse leads me in. Then the nurse says, "Your baby is getting an MRI." And I am. Oh God forgive me, I am relieved. I don't want to see the baby. I could have spent my whole day washing my hands. I go back to Carolyn. Two doctors come in to see us.

ANIL. This was a vaginal delivery, thirty-two weeks. Four pounds two ounces. Seventeen inches long. Baby girl Goldenhersch born with *apgar* score of five. Shortly after birth the baby exhibited signs of cyanosis and was subsequently diagnosed with d-transposition. A Rashkind procedure or a transcatheter balloon atrial septostomy was performed by myself, under the supervision of my senior attending. This is a report. A report which I prepared for the Morbidity and Mortality meeting, the week following the death of the Goldenhersch baby. Under my hands a baby dies. There are others around, supervising, helping. An incalculable error, but my hands, my loss. It isn't easy. But the report for the Morbidity and Mortality meeting is simple. The facts of the case are presented and questions are asked. Questions to clarify details, questions to try to better understand the cause of death — discussions follow. What could have been done differently and more importantly, for me, what should have been done differently. A delicate catheterization and an embolism. Too much bleeding. A septal tear. A balloon-fragment embolism. The details, for you, the details for you aren't so important.

CAROLYN. I never told Michael the reason that I hated the name Virginia so much. When I was little, my mother used "Virginia" as a euphemism for "vagina." My mother is a prude. An awful prude. During my stay at the hospital, she stopped in and when I went to the bathroom, she admonished me for having on a hospital gown that allowed you to see my ass. She tried to cover it up. We didn't know what was happening to the baby yet. She said, "Mommy, I can see your bottom." For weeks before, she had been calling me "Mommy." She was either passing the torch, or making fun of me, I don't know which. After the baby died, she started calling me Carolyn again. My name sounds so disappointing coming from her lips. I know she thinks we failed. That we didn't do it right. Still, our friends, our families, they don't think that we ever even had a baby. Because until it's named and moved into its nursery, it's still property of the pre-parenthood ether. You aren't a parent, I guess, until you get that baby on your own turf.

ANIL. Carolyn Goldenhersch is alone in her post-delivery room. I say to her, without the other doctors around. I say: Mrs. Goldenhersch, I'm sorry, we did everything we could. Your baby died of an embolism shortly after her catheterization. We did everything we could to resuscitate her, but the blood filled her lungs and we couldn't. I'm sorry.

CAROLYN. Were you there?

ANIL. Yes.

CAROLYN. Did she cry?

ANIL. No.

MICHAEL. I'm sitting at the kitchen table, two days after the baby has died. I've got a pen in my hand, I'm going to do the crossword puzzle. I'm ready to do the puzzle. I stare at the front page and words start to pop out. Like the paper is speaking to me. I know it's weird. So, I circle them. I circle words like "death" and "hardship" and "we" and "heal" and "storm." All of these words have been placed there for me. This is what I think and then I realize that I need to get ready to go to the hospital to pick up Carolyn. But I want to finish the paper. Finish finding the words that are written for me. I don't think that Carolyn has these kinds of moments, where the universe seemingly steps forward to comfort her. That the words, while I know that they weren't really put there for me, are enough to get me in the shower. The universe conspires and I am ready to pick up my wife at the hospital after the loss of our baby. And a month or so later, I hope the universe will come to my aid again, so I ask: Should I go with you?

CAROLYN. Where?

MICHAEL. To meet Dr. Patel? To learn about the heart?

CAROLYN. Do you want to?

MICHAEL. I want to be with you.

CAROLYN. Then come.

MICHAEL. Okay.

CAROLYN. I'll ask him.

MICHAEL. You need his permission?

CAROLYN. When he's available. Ask him when he's available to meet us.

MICHAEL. Okay.

CAROLYN. Okay.

MICHAEL. Good. I'll go with you. We'll go together.

CAROLYN. I don't think I'll ever want to have another baby, Michael.

MICHAEL. Why are you saying that?

CAROLYN. Isn't that why you're hanging around?

MICHAEL. No.

CAROLYN. Then why are you here?

MICHAEL. Do you have any idea what you're like?

CAROLYN. Yes.

MICHAEL. Then stop.

CAROLYN. No.

MICHAEL. Grow up.

CAROLYN. Excuse me?

MICHAEL. *(He goes to her.)* This happened to me too! *(She grabs his hand and puts it on her stomach.)*

CAROLYN. What? This?! This happened to you?! *(She throws her arms up and he keeps his hand, awkwardly on her stomach. She looks at his hand. She jumps back. His hand remains mid-air.)* Don't touch me. Don't ever touch me. *(He starts to leave.)* Are you leaving? *(He stops.)* I want you to. I want you to get the hell out.

MICHAEL. No you don't.

CAROLYN. I hate this apartment.

MICHAEL. Then let's move.

CAROLYN. Let's fight.

MICHAEL. We're fighting Carolyn.

CAROLYN. No. I mean, let's really fight.

MICHAEL. Are you going to lay down ground rules?

CAROLYN. You can hit me.

MICHAEL. I don't want to.

CAROLYN. I think you do.

MICHAEL. Let's leave New York.

CAROLYN. And go where?

MICHAEL. I don't know, we could go anywhere. L.A.?

CAROLYN. I can't live in L.A.

MICHAEL. Anywhere you want, Carolyn. I'd go anywhere.

CAROLYN. What about your job?

MICHAEL. I can get another job.

CAROLYN. I'd rather fight.

MICHAEL. Come on, Carolyn, we built our life. It took us, what, five years to get to this place. Five years and then in a month, it's unraveled. Are children that wonderful? Are babies that important?

ANIL. We could pick up takeout.

CAROLYN. I've not not thought about this moment. I've thought about it a lot. But I don't ever decide how it is that we arrive here. Do I say, "Yes, take me to your apartment."

ANIL. Do you want to cab it or subway?

CAROLYN. Do I say, "No. Dr. Patel. I'm not that kind of girl." I could simply look him in the eyes and shake my head. I could turn on my heel and just walk away. I could say, "What about my husband, you may not respect him, but I do." I could spit in his face. I could leave. I could. I could tell him, "I'm sorry, but I can't." That I don't know how I've gotten to this place. That I miss being pregnant. That I don't know how not to have the baby I've been expecting to have and while I'm glad he's into me, I just don't think it's fair because I'm feeling so unstable. I could say, "Let's just have dinner at the restaurant and end our friendship in public. I'm ready to move on."

ANIL. Subway or cab?

CAROLYN. Cab.

MICHAEL. We didn't have a formal funeral service. I've been saying Kaddish every day. I say it not because I believe it, but because I believe that if I say it, I will have done something right. The world doesn't want it to be bad for us. I want Carolyn to say Kaddish with me but she won't.

CAROLYN. God is dead.

MICHAEL. How very undergrad philosophy major of you.

CAROLYN. I'm not playing your religion-in-a-time-of-need game.

MICHAEL. We are actually Jewish, Carolyn.

CAROLYN. What do Hindus do when people die?

ANIL. What do Hindus do?

CAROLYN. How do you mourn?

ANIL. I'm an atheist.

CAROLYN. Come on. Please.

ANIL. Some Hindus shave their heads.

CAROLYN. Really, why?

ANIL. I don't know.

CAROLYN. What else?

ANIL. Cremation. And people bring fruit. When my grandmother died, people brought fruit.

CAROLYN. Why do you think they shave their heads?

ANIL. I don't know.

CAROLYN. I want you to find out for me.

ANIL. You have beautiful hair.

CAROLYN. And he's right. No, seriously, I'm one of those women, sure, I'm good looking enough, but I have great hair. It's new. It came when I got pregnant. I don't know, maybe all of the folic acid. Does it have any thing to do with hair follicles, folic acid? Hair follicles?

ANIL. *(He holds up a book.)* And so the next day, I buy a book. *Teach Yourself Hinduism.* "Chapter One: Diversity and Unity."

CAROLYN. Baby Goldenhersch gave me Rapunzelesque tresses. Dr. Anil Patel, maybe he will rescue me.

MICHAEL. In my adult life, the longest I have ever not been in love is one month. This is true. I have never not been in a relationship and even when those relationships ended, it has never taken me more than a month to fall in love with someone else. I always fall in love on the first date. Sitting across the table from a woman I've just met, in those times that I dated, I could always say to myself, "I love this woman." So, a month after our baby dies, when it seems clear that Carolyn has fallen out of love with me, I begin to wonder, where is she channeling it? Who is getting this displaced love.

CAROLYN. We take a cab. Dr. Anil Patel's apartment is practically above the deli where he gets his morning coffee. It's a New York small apartment. It smells American. I expected it to smell like sandalwood. He makes me tea.

ANIL. Milk?

CAROLYN. Is it chai?

ANIL. Lipton's.

CAROLYN. Yes. Milk is fine.

ANIL. There is a picture of my parents on the window sill. You'll like it.

CAROLYN. They look so young.

ANIL. They were young. My mother is barely nineteen, my father is twenty-five.

CAROLYN. You look like your mother.

ANIL. Do I?

CAROLYN. She's beautiful.

ANIL. Thank you.

CAROLYN. You're beautiful.

ANIL. Carolyn Goldenhersch.

CAROLYN. Dr. Anil Patel.

ANIL. Go home.

CAROLYN. And of course. Of course. *(Carolyn and Anil kiss.)*

ANIL. Carolyn Goldenhersch doesn't stay the night.

CAROLYN. —

ANIL. But she doesn't leave after I've told her to go home.

CAROLYN. No.

ANIL. She doesn't leave right away.

CAROLYN. No.

ANIL. Not until about one in the morning. And I'm a good sleeper, but after she goes, I don't sleep. I have a full sized bed. The whole night, I don't move to the center where she's been. I ask her to, but Carolyn Goldenhersch doesn't stay the night.

CAROLYN. No.

MICHAEL. Who is getting this displaced love? And then, she comes home. At one in the morning. I won't lie and say I was waiting up for her. But I know that it's one because I wake up when she gets into bed. And I'll be honest again, I don't ask her where she's been. I don't. I say, "Are you tired?"

CAROLYN. Yes.

MICHAEL. Then let's go to sleep.

CAROLYN. Okay.

MICHAEL. For the first time in over two months — longer than that — she slides close to me. And we grope, I know that it's graphic, but we grope like teenagers, kind of fumbling and we don't have sex. This is more intimate than that. When we're finally falling asleep, she's all cuddled in next to me and I think that maybe I was wrong. She does still love me.

ANIL. When I got out of bed, the morning after Carolyn came over, I took a shower. I steamed up the bathroom to shave, I wiped the steam off the bathroom mirror and I had a pimple. I laughed. Out loud in my bathroom by myself. I never laugh by myself.

MICHAEL. *(He smiles.)* I used to be a classic TV buff. I would go to the Museum of Television and Radio and watch shows from the fifties. I came across one show. Edgar Bergen was the host, with his sidekick dummy Charlie McCarthy. The show was called *Do You Trust Your Wife*. It ran for seven years. It's where Johnny Carson got his start. *Do You Trust Your Wife*. A game show. *Do You Trust Your Wife*. Entertainment.

CAROLYN. Michael cleared the apartment of baby things before I came home from the hospital. Did it because he wanted to help. I know he did, I know he does. I want him to. I do.

ANIL. *(He reads his book.)* "Chapter Two: The Temple." I think of Mount Sinai. I think of a hospital with a biblical name. The place where Moses found the Ten Commandments. Sacred to the Jews. What am I doing here? Late, on a Friday night, I am sitting in a small visitor's lounge.

CAROLYN. And so, right now, here. Here they are. Here we are. Ha. Here we go. *(Carolyn has the heart in her hands. She breathes in and places the heart on the table before them.)*

MICHAEL. No hot date?

CAROLYN. Michael.

MICHAEL. Friday night.

CAROLYN. We get it.

ANIL. No, no hot date.

CAROLYN. No shabbas dinner?

MICHAEL. Ha. Cute.

ANIL. I'm sorry, if you want —

MICHAEL. No, it's fine.

ANIL. I just thought I should sit —

MICHAEL. In the middle, right. You're fine.

ANIL. So, I can show —

CAROLYN. I'll sit —

MICHAEL. Good. Show us both. Sit. *(Anil sits in the middle chair. Carolyn sits next to*
him. Michael remains standing.)

CAROLYN. Yes, sit.

MICHAEL. This view is so wasted.

ANIL. You can see most of the park.

MICHAEL. People would pay millions to have this view. It's wasted on this room.

ANIL. It's a nice diversion.

MICHAEL. It's hard to believe that people on this floor can be diverted.

CAROLYN. Sit.

MICHAEL. Heel.

CAROLYN. Michael.

ANIL. Have you been looking at the heart?

MICHAEL. No.

CAROLYN. Yes.

MICHAEL. Carolyn's always been an A-student.

CAROLYN. Don't make fun of me.

MICHAEL. You don't think it's a good thing? I bet Dr. Patel thinks it's a good thing.

ANIL. Anil, you can call me Anil.

MICHAEL. Is that what Carolyn calls you?

ANIL. Yes. This model is a bit smaller than scale.

MICHAEL. Are you an A-student?

ANIL. I'm not in school anymore.

MICHAEL. Oh, I thought you were a fellow.

ANIL. Yes, I have received this fellowship, but I am not graded. It's a training program.

MICHAEL. Isn't a training program school?

CAROLYN. Are you going to let us start?

MICHAEL. —

ANIL. Your heart is about the size of your fist. Make a fist. *(Carolyn and Anil make fists.)* Please, Mr. Goldenhersch, to illustrate. *(Michael makes a fist. To Carolyn:)* That is the size of your heart. Your baby's heart, when she was born, it was — Your baby was small.

CAROLYN. Four pounds. Two ounces.

ANIL. Four pounds. Two ounces.

MICHAEL. Small.

CAROLYN. Michael can't wrap his mind around how small.

MICHAEL. Yes I can.

CAROLYN. No you can't.

ANIL. If I stretch out my hand, palm open, like this. *(They all unclench their fists, following Anil's lead, they slowly open their hands, fingers outstretched in almost a waving position.)* From the tip of my middle finger to the tip of my thumb is how big the trunk of your baby's body was at birth. Her heart, the size, essentially, of the pad of my thumb.

MICHAEL. Small.

CAROLYN. Yes, Michael, small. *(They lower their hands.)*

ANIL. It is the heart's job to move blood through the body. Normally, once blood has traveled through the body, it returns — un-oxygenated — to the heart where it passes from the right atrium to the right ventricle then is pumped through the pulmonary artery into the lungs where it receives oxygen. This now oxygenated blood returns from the lungs into the left atrium to the left ventricle and is pumped through the aorta to the body. In transposition, the aorta and the pulmonary artery are switched, or transposed. The aorta is wrongly connected to the right ventricle and the pulmonary artery is wrongly connected to the left.. Two separate loops are created, one that pumps unoxygenated blood from the body back into the body. And one that recirculates oxygenated blood from the lungs back into the lungs. While the baby is in-utero she receives oxygen from the mother, but once the baby is born —

MICHAEL. Her heart didn't breathe.

ANIL. The heart doesn't exactly breathe.

CAROLYN. I think he's being poetic.

MICHAEL. No I'm not. I'm trying to understand it.

ANIL. In a healthy heart like yours —

MICHAEL. Do you hear that Carolyn? A *healthy* heart like mine —

ANIL. Or Carolyn's —

MICHAEL. Is that your professional opinion?

ANIL. I'm sorry?

MICHAEL. Carolyn's heart used to skip beats.

ANIL. Is that so?

MICHAEL. Every time I walked in the room.

ANIL. I see.

CAROLYN. He's putting on a show.

ANIL. Your baby's heart, let me try to explain —

CAROLYN. She wasn't getting enough oxygen. To her blood. She didn't have enough oxygen in her blood.

ANIL. Yes, exactly.

MICHAEL. Teacher's pet.

CAROLYN. *(Referring to the heart.)* So, the blood enters here.

ANIL. *(Taking apart the heart model.)* Yes, the blood normally enters here.

MICHAEL. How long is this going to take?

ANIL. Your wife wants to know.

MICHAEL. I know she does.

ANIL. The Rashkind procedure is a palliative measure. Oxygen levels must be safe, pulmonary and cardiac function must be stabilized before the transposition can be surgically corrected. In the Rashkind procedure, a balloon catheter is passed from a leg vein —

MICHAEL. Where are the other visitors?

ANIL. Who?

MICHAEL. This is a visitor's lounge, isn't it?

ANIL. Yes.

MICHAEL. You don't have an office?

ANIL. I thought this would be more comfortable.

MICHAEL. More comfortable.

ANIL. Yes. And private.

MICHAEL. A private visitor's lounge?

ANIL. Yes.

MICHAEL. So, the heart, it just floats in the body?

ANIL. It's all connected.

MICHAEL. I know. What protects it?

ANIL. Your bones. Your muscles. The pericardium. The heart is strong.

MICHAEL. Are you from New York?

ANIL. I'm sorry?

MICHAEL. Are you a native New Yorker?

ANIL. No. I'm from Connecticut.

MICHAEL. Your parents must be proud.

ANIL. How so?

MICHAEL. A doctor.

ANIL. Yes.

CAROLYN. Michael, your parents are proud of you.

MICHAEL. I didn't say they weren't.

ANIL. I think they wished I had been an engineer.

MICHAEL. Why?

ANIL. I don't know. I have a couple of cousins who are engineers.

MICHAEL. Funny, I have a couple of cousins who are doctors.

CAROLYN. And I have a couple of cousins in real estate. Can we please keep learning about the heart.

MICHAEL. I don't think I want to.

CAROLYN. What?

MICHAEL. I'm not interested. Or I can't wrap my mind around the anatomy. It doesn't register.

ANIL. It's complicated. I can try to simplify —

CAROLYN. Don't you want to know?

MICHAEL. I drive a car and I don't know how an engine works.

CAROLYN. You aren't seriously comparing the heart and knowing how your body functions to a car.

ANIL. Actually, it's a good comparison.

CAROLYN. Don't encourage him.

MICHAEL. I trust that someone else knows. That when my car breaks down I can take it to a mechanic and he'll fix it.

CAROLYN. And if you have a heart attack, if you are lying in your hospital bed and your doctor is explaining the procedures, don't you want to know what he or she is talking about?

MICHAEL. No. I'll trust that the doctor knows and will fix it.

CAROLYN. And if the mechanic doesn't fix your car. If he doesn't get it right?

MICHAEL. I'll get a new mechanic. A better one.

CAROLYN. And if your heart fails? If the doctor doesn't get it right?

MICHAEL. I'll die.

CAROLYN. You'll die.

MICHAEL. Yes.

CAROLYN. That's it?

MICHAEL. If I understand the procedure and the doctor doesn't get it right, what difference does it make.

ANIL. I understood the procedure. I understand it.

MICHAEL. Is this what we're here for? Absolution?

ANIL. I don't need forgiveness.

MICHAEL. I think you do.

CAROLYN. Who would absolve him, Michael, you?

MICHAEL. I don't forgive him. Do you?

CAROLYN. Forgive him for what?

ANIL. I am not guilty of anything.

MICHAEL. Bullshit.

CAROLYN. Michael —

MICHAEL. Bullshit. Bullshit. Bullshit.

ANIL. I take responsibility for my actions, but —

MICHAEL. But you're not guilty —

ANIL. No.

MICHAEL. How the hell do you live with yourself?

ANIL. I'm sorry for your loss. Unfortunate things happen.

CAROLYN. We're not here to place blame —

MICHAEL. Isn't that what this is? Don't you blame me?

CAROLYN. Michael, this isn't the time —

MICHAEL. Isn't it?

ANIL. Your wife is a nice woman —

MICHAEL. Yes, I know, I'm her husband.

ANIL. It is different, for women, the loss of a baby is different.

MICHAEL. Of course it is.

ANIL. For women, after they've carried the fetus for so many months —

MICHAEL. I understand that it's different for women. I'm not an idiot.

CAROLYN. Don't do this, talk about me like I'm not here.

MICHAEL. Don't worry, we know you're here. You're the connection. You have to be here.

CAROLYN. I have to be here.

MICHAEL. Do I have to be here?

CAROLYN. You said you wanted to come with me to learn.

MICHAEL. I'm not so sure Dr. Patel's such a good teacher.

ANIL. As part of my training, I teach other doctors, I've never had any complaints —

MICHAEL. What is the saying, "Learn one, do one — "

ANIL. It's *see* one, do one, teach one.

MICHAEL. And Dr. Patel you did one.

ANIL. *(To Carolyn.)* Maybe we should look at the heart —

CAROLYN. Michael, you asked to come.

MICHAEL. Should I leave you two alone to teach my wife?

ANIL. Your wife asked me to come.

CAROLYN. Michael, don't you want to be here?

MICHAEL. I want to be with you.

CAROLYN. I know.

MICHAEL. And you want to be with me?

CAROLYN. Yes, yes, I do.

ANIL. Carolyn.

MICHAEL. What does he want?

CAROLYN. He's a doctor.

MICHAEL. Why this doctor?

CAROLYN. Because he knows.

MICHAEL. What does he know?

ANIL. This is my specialty.

MICHAEL. Mistakes are your specialty?

ANIL. There was an error made, yes, but I —

MICHAEL. Not a mistake.

ANIL. Not in the way that you think of it.

MICHAEL. And what way do I think of it?

ANIL. Carolyn understands.

MICHAEL. What does she understand? Why we're here? What

45

mistake, I'm sorry, error Dr. Patel made?

CAROLYN. Michael, stop.

MICHAEL. Now you want to stop?

CAROLYN. That's all I want. A moment of stopping.

ANIL. We should all just take a deep breath. Stop —

MICHAEL. Do you think we should meditate? Hold hands and reflect?

ANIL. I believe that Carolyn wants a moment.

MICHAEL. I don't think that's what she wants.

CAROLYN. I want you to understand what happened.

MICHAEL. And if I understand what happened, then we'll be done here? Water under the bridge.

ANIL. I've seen parents move on.

MICHAEL. And Anil, what about you, what happens to you, you get back on the saddle? Continue to ruin lives?

CAROLYN. Why are you such an asshole?

MICHAEL. I'm the asshole? Me? And Anil here, what is he? Krishna come down to save us?

CAROLYN. Oh Jesus, Michael! Anil, I'm sorry —

ANIL. No, I —

MICHAEL. Don't apologize for me —

CAROLYN. And who are you? Job?

MICHAEL. And you? Mary fucking Magdalene?

CAROLYN. Are you calling me a whore?

MICHAEL. Is that what Anil calls you?

ANIL. Hey!

MICHAEL. "Hey" what? Really, what?

CAROLYN. Anil, ignore him. He's —

ANIL. You can't talk to her that way — He's upset, I get it. He's angry.

MICHAEL. And why would I be angry? Because of what you did to our baby? Because of the way you're looking at my wife?

ANIL. I'd say you're angry because of the way your wife is looking at me.

CAROLYN. Don't!

ANIL. Your wife wants to learn —

MICHAEL. See one, do one, fuck my wife?

ANIL. I respect your wife.

MICHAEL. You respect my wife? Are you kidding me?

ANIL. No. I actually respect your wife.

46

MICHAEL. Carolyn?

CAROLYN. We have one little picture, Michael. Snapped with your phone. We weren't prepared.

MICHAEL. No.

CAROLYN. Now, after the fact, we have to prepare ourselves for what has already happened.

MICHAEL. That's impossible.

CAROLYN. I know.

ANIL. I just want to help you.

CAROLYN. I know.

MICHAEL. We didn't mean for anything bad to happen.

CAROLYN. No, I know.

ANIL. Let me, Carolyn. Please.

MICHAEL. I don't know why you keep trying to make something else bad happen. You love me.

CAROLYN. Yes.

MICHAEL. Prepare yourself for that.

ANIL. You love me.

CAROLYN. Yes.

MICHAEL. You love him because you think he killed our baby?

CAROLYN. Yes. *(Michael rises and goes to Anil. Michael stands Anil up. Michael places his hand on Anil's shoulder.)*

MICHAEL. He didn't. He isn't as strong as that would make him. He's a man who made a mistake. An error. Don't move —

ANIL. I'm not afraid of you.

MICHAEL. Not a man strong enough to kill someone. He's not stronger than we are.

CAROLYN. Michael.

MICHAEL. I know how weak you think I am.

CAROLYN. I don't.

MICHAEL. *(Still holding on to Anil, Michael alternates showing his fist to Anil and pounding his fist against his own chest.)* Look at my fist, my heart, my fist, my heart, my fist.

ANIL. I don't want to fight you.

MICHAEL. I don't want to fight you, I want to rip out your heart. Kill you, like you killed our baby. Like you're trying to kill my marriage.

ANIL. Look at your wife.

MICHAEL. Yes, my *wife*.

ANIL. You have to tell him to go or he won't.

CAROLYN. He's my husband.

ANIL. Look how miserable he makes you.

CAROLYN. I am not miserable.

ANIL. Yes you are.

MICHAEL. *(To Anil.)* What did you lose?

ANIL. What did I lose?

MICHAEL. We lost a baby. What did you lose?

ANIL. A patient.

MICHAEL. Tell me you love me.

CAROLYN. I love you.

ANIL. Carolyn, don't do this.

MICHAEL. *I* know how you feel. *He* doesn't.

ANIL. Yes, I do. I'm trying.

MICHAEL. You don't love him.

ANIL. I'm sorry, I'm sorry, but she does. I think she definitely does.

CAROLYN. Yes, I think I do.

ANIL. I know you do.

MICHAEL. Should I hit him? Should I, Carolyn? Should I leave?

CAROLYN. You can't leave Michael. This isn't so clean.

MICHAEL. You can't love him.

ANIL. Yes, she can.

CAROLYN. I can't. I can't love him, I can't love you.

MICHAEL. Can't?

ANIL. She's saying she wants to love but can't.

MICHAEL. Yes, she's speaking English, I understand English.

CAROLYN. This is not the moment where I break down. I am not broken.

ANIL. No one is saying you're broken, Carolyn —

MICHAEL. Are you comforting her?

ANIL. I'm trying to, yes.

CAROLYN. I don't need to be comforted.

MICHAEL. What do you need?

CAROLYN. Our baby.

MICHAEL. Then let's have another baby.

CAROLYN. Not *another* baby.

MICHAEL. And you think he can give you that?

ANIL. I love you.

MICHAEL. Shut the fuck up.

ANIL. Do you hear me? I love you, Carolyn Goldenhersch.

CAROLYN. I know and it isn't enough.

MICHAEL. I know you are not this woman who does such awful things.

CAROLYN. I think I am.

ANIL. You aren't doing anything awful.

CAROLYN. I should have done it better, I know, I should have done it better, but I can't —

MICHAEL. — don't say that —

CAROLYN. — I should have kept her breathing, carried her to term —

MICHAEL. — you didn't make this happen, it just happened, it's awful and it happened —

CAROLYN. — I should have done it right, I shouldn't have walked around so much, I should have eaten more, I should have been more careful, I should have made sure —

MICHAEL. — I should have helped you —

CAROLYN. — rested more, I should have done it right. I should have saved her. I wasn't good enough. I could have done something. If she weren't born early — should have kept her in —

ANIL. It wouldn't have made a difference.

CAROLYN. No, no I know.

MICHAEL. Carolyn, please. I'm sorry, please, I need you please, I need you, please, you need me too.

CAROLYN. A baby called "baby" can never be anything more than that. Not your child. Just something that you've wanted to love.

MICHAEL. And that's my fault?

CAROLYN. Yes.

ANIL. And mine?

CAROLYN. Yes and mine.

MICHAEL. Look at me.

CAROLYN. Our baby dies. *(She looks to Michael, to Anil, then to the audience.)* Our baby dies, our baby dies, our baby diesourbaby-diedourbabydies* — Maybe I should be comforted by the fact that this will be the worst thing that will ever happen to me. Maybe I can make something worse happen. Maybe I did. *(She stands.)* This should be over, shouldn't it? *(She moves closer to the audience. The men are now at a distance. She looks back at them. One last time.)* A couple of years ago, my best friend had an affair with a CPA her husband worked with. For two months, she and I talked every morning. Early. While she was driving her kids to school. I told Michael about it. He said, "Why are you trying to comfort her? She's doing something wrong." I said, "I'm comforting her *because* she's doing something wrong." My head hurts. I think there is too much time in a day. *(Carolyn becomes part of her audience.)* I'm sorry. *(Blackout.)*

End of Play

PROPERTY LIST

Plastic model of human heart
Book on Hinduism

NEW PLAYS

★ **GUARDIANS by Peter Morris.** In this unflinching look at war, a disgraced American soldier discloses the truth about Abu Ghraib prison, and a clever English journalist reveals how he faked a similar story for the London tabloids. "Compelling, sympathetic and powerful." *–NY Times.* "Sends you into a state of moral turbulence." *–Sunday Times (UK).* "Nothing short of remarkable." *–Village Voice.* [1M, 1W] ISBN: 978-0-8222-2177-7

★ **BLUE DOOR by Tanya Barfield.** Three generations of men (all played by one actor), from slavery through Black Power, challenge Lewis, a tenured professor of mathematics, to embark on a journey combining past and present. "A teasing flare for words." *–Village Voice.* "Unfailingly thought-provoking." *–LA Times.* "The play moves with the speed and logic of a dream." *–Seattle Weekly.* [2M] ISBN: 978-0-8222-2209-5

★ **THE INTELLIGENT DESIGN OF JENNY CHOW by Rolin Jones.** This irreverent "techno-comedy" chronicles one brilliant woman's quest to determine her heritage and face her fears with the help of her astounding creation called Jenny Chow. "Boldly imagined." *–NY Times.* "Fantastical and funny." *–Variety.* "Harvests many laughs and finally a few tears." *–LA Times.* [3M, 3W] ISBN: 978-0-8222-2071-8

★ **SOUVENIR by Stephen Temperley.** Florence Foster Jenkins, a wealthy society eccentric, suffers under the delusion that she is a great coloratura soprano—when in fact the opposite is true. "Hilarious and deeply touching. Incredibly moving and breathtaking." *–NY Daily News.* "A sweet love letter of a play." *–NY Times.* "Wildly funny. Completely charming." *–Star-Ledger.* [1M, 1W] ISBN: 978-0-8222-2157-9

★ **ICE GLEN by Joan Ackermann.** In this touching period comedy, a beautiful poetess dwells in idyllic obscurity on a Berkshire estate with a band of unlikely cohorts. "A beautifully written story of nature and change." *–Talkin' Broadway.* "A lovely play which will leave you with a lot to think about." *–CurtainUp.* "Funny, moving and witty." *–Metroland (Boston).* [4M, 3W] ISBN: 978-0-8222-2175-3

★ **THE LAST DAYS OF JUDAS ISCARIOT by Stephen Adly Guirgis.** Set in a time-bending, darkly comic world between heaven and hell, this play reexamines the plight and fate of the New Testament's most infamous sinner. "An unforced eloquence that finds the poetry in lowdown street talk." *–NY Times.* "A real jaw-dropper." *–Variety.* "An extraordinary play." *–Guardian (UK).* [10M, 5W] ISBN: 978-0-8222-2082-4

DRAMATISTS PLAY SERVICE, INC.
440 Park Avenue South, New York, NY 10016 212-683-8960 Fax 212-213-1539
postmaster@dramatists.com www.dramatists.com

NEW PLAYS

★ **THE GREAT AMERICAN TRAILER PARK MUSICAL music and lyrics by David Nehls, book by Betsy Kelso.** Pippi, a stripper on the run, has just moved into Armadillo Acres, wreaking havoc among the tenants of Florida's most exclusive trailer park. "Adultery, strippers, murderous ex-boyfriends, Costco and the Ice Capades. Undeniable fun." –*NY Post.* "Joyful and unashamedly vulgar." –*The New Yorker.* "Sparkles with treasure." –*New York Sun.* [2M, 5W] ISBN: 978-0-8222-2137-1

★ **MATCH by Stephen Belber.** When a young Seattle couple meet a prominent New York choreographer, they are led on a fraught journey that will change their lives forever. "Uproariously funny, deeply moving, enthralling theatre." –*NY Daily News.* "Prolific laughs and ear-to-ear smiles." –*NY Magazine.* [2M, 1W] ISBN: 978-0-8222-2020-6

★ **MR. MARMALADE by Noah Haidle.** Four-year-old Lucy's imaginary friend, Mr. Marmalade, doesn't have much time for her—not to mention he has a cocaine addiction and a penchant for pornography. "Alternately hilarious and heartbreaking." –*The New Yorker.* "A mature and accomplished play." –*LA Times.* "Scathingly observant comedy." –*Miami Herald.* [4M, 2W] ISBN: 978-0-8222-2142-5

★ **MOONLIGHT AND MAGNOLIAS by Ron Hutchinson.** Three men cloister themselves as they work tirelessly to reshape a screenplay that's just not working—*Gone with the Wind.* "Consumers of vintage Hollywood insider stories will eat up Hutchinson's diverting conjecture." –*Variety.* "A lot of fun." –*NY Post.* "A Hollywood dream-factory farce." –*Chicago Sun-Times.* [3M, 1W] ISBN: 978-0-8222-2084-8

★ **THE LEARNED LADIES OF PARK AVENUE by David Grimm, translated and freely adapted from Molière's *Les Femmes Savantes.*** Dicky wants to marry Betty, but her mother's plan is for Betty to wed a most pompous man. "A brave, brainy and barmy revision." –*Hartford Courant.* "A rare but welcome bird in contemporary theatre." –*New Haven Register.* "Roll over Cole Porter." –*Boston Globe.* [5M, 5W] ISBN: 978-0-8222-2135-7

★ **REGRETS ONLY by Paul Rudnick.** A sparkling comedy of Manhattan manners that explores the latest topics in marriage, friendships and squandered riches. "One of the funniest quip-meisters on the planet." –*NY Times.* "Precious moments of hilarity. Devastatingly accurate political and social satire." –*BackStage.* "Great fun." –*CurtainUp.* [3M, 3W] ISBN: 978-0-8222-2223-1

DRAMATISTS PLAY SERVICE, INC.
440 Park Avenue South, New York, NY 10016 212-683-8960 Fax 212-213-1539
postmaster@dramatists.com www.dramatists.com

NEW PLAYS

★ **RABBIT HOLE by David Lindsay-Abaire.** Winner of the 2007 Pulitzer Prize. Becca and Howie Corbett have everything a couple could want until a life-shattering accident turns their world upside down. "An intensely emotional examination of grief, laced with wit." —*Variety.* "A transcendent and deeply affecting new play." —*Entertainment Weekly.* "Painstakingly beautiful." —*BackStage.* [2M, 3W] ISBN: 978-0-8222-2154-8

★ **DOUBT, A Parable by John Patrick Shanley.** Winner of the 2005 Pulitzer Prize and Tony Award. Sister Aloysius, a Bronx school principal, takes matters into her own hands when she suspects the young Father Flynn of improper relations with one of the male students. "All the elements come invigoratingly together like clockwork." —*Variety.* "Passionate, exquisite, important, engrossing." —*NY Newsday.* [1M, 3W] ISBN: 978-0-8222-2219-4

★ **THE PILLOWMAN by Martin McDonagh.** In an unnamed totalitarian state, an author of horrific children's stories discovers that someone has been making his stories come true. "A blindingly bright black comedy." —*NY Times.* "McDonagh's least forgiving, bravest play." —*Variety.* "Thoroughly startling and genuinely intimidating." —*Chicago Tribune.* [4M, 5 bit parts (2M, 1W, 1 boy, 1 girl)] ISBN: 978-0-8222-2100-5

★ **GREY GARDENS book by Doug Wright, music by Scott Frankel, lyrics by Michael Korie.** The hilarious and heartbreaking story of Big Edie and Little Edie Bouvier Beale, the eccentric aunt and cousin of Jacqueline Kennedy Onassis, once bright names on the social register who became East Hampton's most notorious recluses. "An experience no passionate theatergoer should miss." —*NY Times.* "A unique and unmissable musical." —*Rolling Stone.* [4M, 3W, 2 girls] ISBN: 978-0-8222-2181-4

★ **THE LITTLE DOG LAUGHED by Douglas Carter Beane.** Mitchell Green could make it big as the hot new leading man in Hollywood if Diane, his agent, could just keep him in the closet. "Devastatingly funny." —*NY Times.* "An out-and-out delight." —*NY Daily News.* "Full of wit and wisdom." —*NY Post.* [2M, 2W] ISBN: 978-0-8222-2226-2

★ **SHINING CITY by Conor McPherson.** A guilt-ridden man reaches out to a therapist after seeing the ghost of his recently deceased wife. "Haunting, inspired and glorious." —*NY Times.* "Simply breathtaking and astonishing." —*Time Out.* "A thoughtful, artful, absorbing new drama." —*Star-Ledger.* [3M, 1W] ISBN: 978-0-8222-2187-6

DRAMATISTS PLAY SERVICE, INC.
440 Park Avenue South, New York, NY 10016 212-683-8960 Fax 212-213-1539
postmaster@dramatists.com www.dramatists.com

NEW PLAYS

★ **AFTER ASHLEY by Gina Gionfriddo.** A teenager is unwillingly thrust into the national spotlight when a family tragedy becomes talk-show fodder. "A work that virtually any audience would find accessible." –*NY Times.* "Deft characterization and caustic humor." –*NY Sun.* "A smart satirical drama." –*Variety.* [4M, 2W] ISBN: 978-0-8222-2099-2

★ **THE RUBY SUNRISE by Rinne Groff.** Twenty-five years after Ruby struggles to realize her dream of inventing the first television, her daughter faces similar battles of faith as she works to get Ruby's story told on network TV. "Measured and intelligent, optimistic yet clear-eyed." –*NY Magazine.* "Maintains an exciting sense of ingenuity." –*Village Voice.* "Sinuous theatrical flair." –*Broadway.com.* [3M, 4W] ISBN: 978-0-8222-2140-1

★ **MY NAME IS RACHEL CORRIE taken from the writings of Rachel Corrie, edited by Alan Rickman and Katharine Viner.** This solo piece tells the story of Rachel Corrie who was killed in Gaza by an Israeli bulldozer set to demolish a Palestinian home. "Heartbreaking urgency. An invigoratingly detailed portrait of a passionate idealist." –*NY Times.* "Deeply authentically human." –*USA Today.* "A stunning dramatization." –*CurtainUp.* [1W] ISBN: 978-0-8222-2222-4

★ **ALMOST, MAINE by John Cariani.** This charming midwinter night's dream of a play turns romantic clichés on their ear as it chronicles the painfully hilarious amorous adventures (and misadventures) of residents of a remote northern town that doesn't quite exist. "A whimsical approach to the joys and perils of romance." –*NY Times.* "Sweet, poignant and witty." –*NY Daily News.* "Aims for the heart by way of the funny bone." –*Star-Ledger.* [2M, 2W] ISBN: 978-0-8222-2156-2

★ **Mitch Albom's TUESDAYS WITH MORRIE by Jeffrey Hatcher and Mitch Albom, based on the book by Mitch Albom.** The true story of Brandeis University professor Morrie Schwartz and his relationship with his student Mitch Albom. "A touching, life-affirming, deeply emotional drama." –*NY Daily News.* "You'll laugh. You'll cry." –*Variety.* "Moving and powerful." –*NY Post.* [2M] ISBN: 978-0-8222-2188-3

★ **DOG SEES GOD: CONFESSIONS OF A TEENAGE BLOCKHEAD by Bert V. Royal.** An abused pianist and a pyromaniac ex-girlfriend contribute to the teen-angst of America's most hapless kid. "A welcome antidote to the notion that the *Peanuts* gang provides merely American cuteness." –*NY Times.* "Hysterically funny." –*NY Post.* "The *Peanuts* kids have finally come out of their shells." –*Time Out.* [4M, 4W] ISBN: 978-0-8222-2152-4

DRAMATISTS PLAY SERVICE, INC.
440 Park Avenue South, New York, NY 10016 212-683-8960 Fax 212-213-1539
postmaster@dramatists.com *www.dramatists.com*